Interview and job search strategies that work

Interview and Job Search Strategies (that work)

Second Edition

Gary McNeely
&
Marcus Lamb

Amazon Books
Seattle, WA

Preface

Plan your day, month, year.
If you fail to plan, you plan to fail.

What has worked for me is to create a family success plan.

I ask the family, can we sell this? And for anything new, can we make it ourselves? This has worked well as we have since built a kitchen table and bench that serves as a family conference table where we float ideas.

We took an inventory of our finances and projected out 1, 3, 6, 9 and 12 months.
In our family journal, we wrote out what our plans are for earning extra income, and what things we think are needed to do so.

Try starting a journal to document your thoughts, ideas and feelings.

I am grateful you read this book, thank you

Thank you to My wife, my kids, V3 beehive, Mom and Dad, Grandma and Grandpa, the McNeely family, Loretta and Tim, and Jesus Christ.

Gary McNeely
Columbia, MO
GARYMCNEELYIT.TECH

Preface

The concept of intelligence and natural ability has been an interest of mine for some time. I talk to many people who are members of high IQ societies, and believe that worth can be derived from a number with little else to support that assumption. As the years get shorter, and I find myself more inclined to listen rather than expound, I feel I have satisfied my desire to understand the purpose and use of intelligence.

I like to compare knowledge to light a lot in both my writing and thoughts. If the mind were a star then its rays would be wisdom we pass to others. Our Sun is rather average: it is not the biggest or brightest in the universe by far, and yet with it brings all of humanity its hopes, dreams, and ability to persevere to our potential. What good is being the hottest brightest star if you cannot warm anyone with your immensity? You do not have to be the greatest, just the one who is willing to reach out across the void and illuminate something or someone.

I hope that by sharing some of my thoughts and ideas with you that I can add a little warmth to our condition. While I consider this book just a spark of a thing, I hope that it is the one that sets your future aflame with prosperity.

I would like to thank my wife Sarah, my daughter Sophia, and my mother Emma for being the lights in my darkness.

Marcus Lamb
San Antonio, TX

Table of Contents

Chapter 1. Thoughts and Ideas

How do I protect a dream?

A good way to do this is to listen to what you say to yourself and to others. Too often, we repeat negatively charged words out of sheer habit. For instance, if you sprinkle your conversation with would've, could've, should've or gonna, you are negatively charging yourself.

Another thing you don't want to do is kill your dreams before you realize them. The word "but" and all of his family are dream killers. "But" is a word that forces limitations on us. "But" lets us procrastinate and gives us an excuse for not living our dreams. For instance, did you ever say to yourself, "I could have done whatever it was, but... something got in the way"? I know I have. "But" allows us to validate our inaction.

Remember, you need to look for reasons to move forward, not for excuses why you are standing still. If you don't take direct action in life, you will always be reacting to what life throws at you. Take it from me, that is no fun at all.

That is why it is important to listen to yourself, so that you are always positively charging yourself. Here are a few easy things you can do that will keep you on the right path.

Become a human Geiger counter tuned to negative thoughts and words. Listen for the "buts," "could've," "would've," "should've," and "gonnas," and replace them with "I will." Then schedule what you want to do, and do it.

Think about all the times you may have reacted negatively in the past and envision what would have happened if you had acted positively to these situations. Next, think about any current situations where you need to act positively and envision what will happen when you do take positive action.

This week, concentrate on responding only in a positive manner to everyone and everything. Imitate positively charged people you know or have read about. Think about how they would react to whatever situation you find yourself in and do what you think they would do. Don't criticize or judge your actions, just do it.

At the end of the week, write down all the things you accomplished with this new attitude. Do these things and you will stay positively charged? Design or goal templates that will help you to change your job.

To make it as clear as possible, here are a few examples of my goal affirmations. I live in a healthy body:

- Today is a great day.
- I will be super good today.
- I will earn X amount of dollars every second

Write out your major goals every day or design your future, what works for me is putting my tasks into an app called Todoist. I put everything in there, like the things I want to do, be, or have.

- Start with the basic things: everyone has a car or can ride the bus, what can you do in the bus or car that can help you change your life?
- Start with a starting point: replace those things from others that are negative with positive, meaning say what is good about this and write it down the way you would like to see.
- Rewrite an email that is negative and send it to yourself with what you would like to see. If you are mad at someone or something then find a quiet place and yell at that person. You can record it and write down on a piece of paper how many times you got mad that day and what was the cause of your anger and how you reacted. Keep this for later and after each week review the negative events and why you got mad.
- Write down on a piece of paper how much money you would like to see in your bank account. What bank would you like this money located in, what interest rate is your money earning? Go to this bank and ask the banker "how much interest does my money earn, and how much does it cost to keep my money in your bank?"
- Write down on a piece of paper what job you would like, if you have a favorite hobby what does that favorite hobby pay? How long is the commute from the company to your home? What is the dress code? How many employees are at that company? How long have they been in business? Who is their major competitor? What are all of the products they produce? Do they have a work from home policy? Do they have 401k, and if so, who is the provider? Do they send their employees to training and if so, where and for how long and what time of the year? Do they have a laptop purchase reimbursement policy? Do they have company picnics, how many holiday days and sick days do they give every month? Does your manager have a messy desk?

Imagine you work at McDonald's and are a cook or cashier. What skills are there that you can gain for your success.

What can be gained from being a cook? Ask the manager to give you an estimate of how many burgers or breakfast sandwiches and what type are being sold for the hours you work and break it out per hour. Knowing this information will help you to see what is the most amount of breakfast and lunch supplies you need to make available. You now can calculate your pay per product: for example, if you work 7am to 2pm with 30 minutes unpaid lunch, this is 6.5 hours. If the company sold 300 sandwiches between 7am to 8am, and your hourly rate is $8.00 per hour, then your rate per product is 2.6 cents per sandwich.

You ask your manager what the company's cost is for 300 sandwiches. Her response is 3 cents per sandwich. You now know to RESEARCH this one. From here you can start to understand the company and the various resources flows. This information is important if you want to grow both yourself and the company. Knowing information about the various processes and profit producing capabilities of any organization will help you in both your current role and elsewhere if you ever decided to move up or even on to other opportunities.

Some people will read this advice and wonder why a fry cook would even need to know anything more than how to do their job well. Knowing what is expected of you from both your customers and your employer will help you achieve your goals quickly. If you know how much of a product needs to be produced at various times throughout the day then it will put less stress and pressure on you, cause less waste for the company, and maybe that will mean more for you in either bonuses or promotions. Whatever the outcome, learning more about your job will always lead to putting you in a better bargaining position and lend you more avenues for options in the future.

Chapter 2. Your new I.T. Information Technology Career

Wherever you're working, here are several items to identify so that if you move to your next job/career on day 1, you bring value to the company.

- What results does my company expect?

- Why am I on the payroll?

- For every 1 dollar you earn, either from your job or from your business, that is like serving 1 person or solving 1 person's problem 1 time.

- You can use what I call the Candy bar method of tasks (explained below):

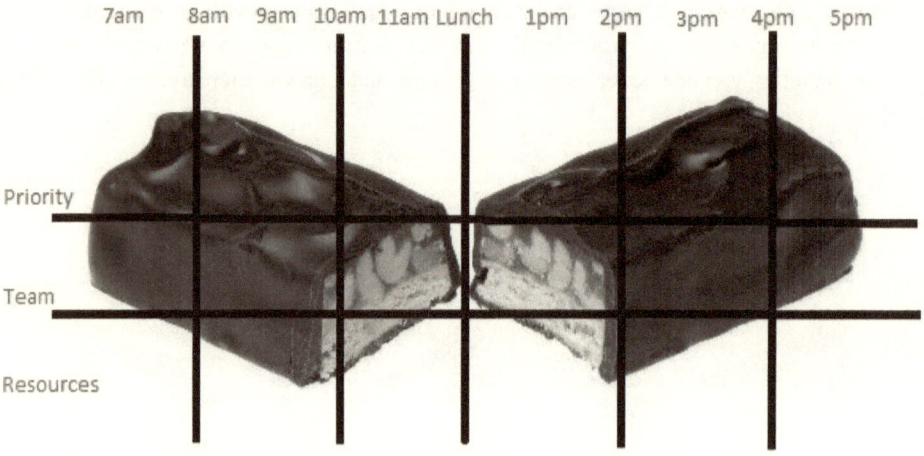

Allow me to explain what I mean about the candy bar method of tasks. Take a candy bar and chop it up left to right into equal pieces. This represents your 8-hour workday. We then go top to bottom representing these 3 things:

1. The priority you put on that block of time, this could be a meeting or a project that is due. An example may be a meeting with management.

2. The team members you will need to work with during that time to get a task complete.

An example is another person's knowledge, maybe to teach me how to do a task but they are only available at a certain time during the day.

3. The resources you will need to get that task complete. An example is if the training room is only available during a certain time during the day.

I use a candy bar to demonstrate what I mean because it is a delicious thought experiment; a simple table could easily demonstrate the same concept, but it does so in a less memorable and less tasty way.

Keeping track of your time and the inputs and outputs of a system is one of the best tools you can wield in architecting your future. In the beginning when you are just starting out and learning these concepts, it will take more time. Once you start to internalize the concepts then they will become second nature to you and, depending on the complexity, you may even forgo having to write everything down or refer back to documents. Of course, if you find yourself becoming too acclimated to your job and the requirements needed to excel, then it may be time to ask for more responsibility and in doing so, give yourself more opportunity to learn even more about the workings of your selected environment.

Getting a job in I.T is not easy but it is not overly difficult. It really depends on what skills you have and who or what is your competition. A running joke in the information technology field is "Do not get me mad or I will replace you with a small script (a script being a piece of code that does a preprogrammed function.)" If you are clear and are focused on what skills you need and what obstacles you may face, then take that focus to someone who is doing what you want to do and just ask them how they did it. You will find no better resource than to ask someone who is doing what you want to do. Maybe record him/her talking about how they started in the IT field and play that over and over. By finding out how they achieved the goals you would also like to attain, you can find ways to bypass working for years just to get to their level. Let me talk about what I mean.

On average a Systems Administrator takes 5-7 years to attain that position and they earn depending on location $80,000 to $130,000 per year.

Here is how you can bypass that 5-7 years.

1. Get your first job in a call center as a telemarketer, you get free training on how to field phone calls. The skills you develop are getting told NO and getting yelled at by customers, teaching you how to fail over and over again. You also learn what methods work well and how to talk to people.
2. While you're working as a telemarketer, put your resume out on the internet and try to get 5 phone interviews per week for a job as a Help Desk technician. What you will learn is what an employer is looking for, and what skills you need to learn. Give yourself 10 hours a week dedicated just to watching YouTube videos or Udemy videos on that skill you need to learn to have your next job.
3. Once you're a Help Desk technician, the skills you will learn are how to handle people's computer problems while they ask is it done yet, so patience is key here.
4. While you're working as a Help Desk technician, put your resume out on the internet and try to get 5 phone interviews per week for a job as a Systems Administrator.
5. Once you're a Systems Administrator, the skills you will learn are those similar to that of a Help Desk technician along with managing servers, creating training documentation, and having input on hardware purchases.

The reason this approach works is because you set easily workable and attainable goals with a timeline. Most people end up doing the same thing (which if fine) because they become comfortable in a position and make a decision not to pursue goals with committed intentions. Any of the previous positions can lead to a happy life but if you want to climb the ladder in IT, or any other field, you have to set goals and timelines and **actively** engage yourself in meeting those goals. Also remember the most important part of all these jobs is the ability to work with, and get along with, people from all walks of life, and understanding their behavior patterns.

Chapter 3. Supplement Reading with How-to Videos

Watching videos is a good strategy to reinforce or even prime a new skill you are trying to learn. While I find videos less dense on how much knowledge they can offer vs. reading (given the same amount of time), I find that a good mix of how-to videos along with related readings will help you get proficient at almost anything you try to pursue. You can try recording yourself reading a book and play it while you try to fall asleep, this works also with rain sounds, 528 Hz frequency, and just about any type of audio designed not to energize. Please note that I am not saying you will learn anything while you sleep, but you can learn something while you are unwinding, like people who read right before bed.

Chapter 4. Meet Lots of People

The reason or the WHY to meet many people, is because you can learn things from them, and they learn things from you. A membership to a gym with a pool is a perfect scenario for this: while the kids swim you can meet someone new. The ideas people share have value, and you get to understand the way another person thinks. You never know who your next best friend is going to be.

Chapter 5. Hoarding 101

If you are a former Hoarder or someone who saves everything like papers and old computers, this solution works for me.

What I do is, with my cell phone, I take a picture of the paper or magazine or device and then I sell it on eBay, throw it in the trash, or take it to goodwill. This way I can send that picture to a friend or post it on a social media site and hope that someone will get value from it.

Chapter 6. Work for Yourself While Working for Your Company

Write down all the employee positions in the company you work for, and estimate their take home salary per year. Now imagine you are the CEO of the company and try to put yourself in that frame of mind and write down all the things you think that goes into making the company money.

- Who are our competitors?
- Why do our customers buy from us?
- Estimate every kind of expense from free coffee to the cost of electricity.
- Write down 10 positive questions and ask yourself these questions 3 times a day for 30 days.
- Find out what you want to do and find out everything about that job.

Start your own LLC Limited liability corporation, come up with a name and get your federal tax id. Once you have these then ask yourself how you can get free stuff from other companies in your field. If you partner with them, does that benefit you and them? Some companies, when you partner with them, will give you access to free sales training and free software.

Chapter 7. I Just Went from Seed to Series A funding.

Walk with me inside a situation you may find yourself in one day.

Congratulations, the high demand for your product and its value in the marketplace means you will have to hire more people, get a bigger facility and start asking people outside your company to invest.

Fast forward 2 months and the company MeshedTechs Software just went through seed and series A funding.

Investors gave your company 3 million dollars, of course they have trust in your judgement in running the company (at least until you ask for more money).

The company makes software that will create holograms from home videos. The software gives families a chance to talk to a forgotten loved one.

You as the CTO or chief technical officer, figure out it will take another 51 people (currently 9) to get you to sell enough software licenses to turn the 3-million-dollar loan into a 9-million-dollar profit within the first 3 years.

Listed are the things you will need:

1. Enough office space for 60 highly skilled employees to work
2. Lease agreement for an office space large enough for 60 employees
3. Office furniture for those 60 employees
4. Computer equipment and Internet service into the building
5. Interview and hire 45 extra highly skilled programmers
6. Interview and hire 6 excellent sales professionals
7. Purchase a service that allows for the backup and restore of company data
8. Pay your 60-person staff a salary for the year
9. DON'T spend all the money in the first 4 quarters. (1 year)

Enough office space for 60 highly skilled employees to work

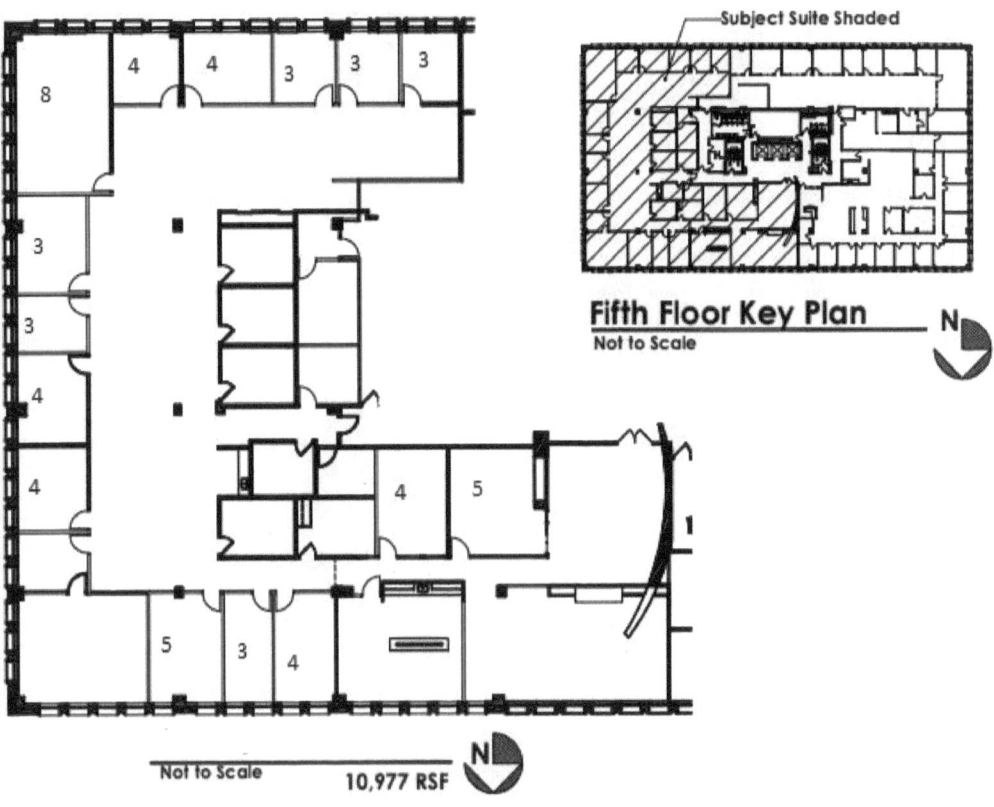

Subject Suite Shaded

Fifth Floor Key Plan
Not to Scale

Not to Scale   10,977 RSF

Total cost of building for the first year $ 192,108.00

                                                    -$3,000,000.00

                                                    $2,807,892.00

Lease agreement for an office space large enough for 60 employees

Office Space Lease

This Lease Agreement (this "Lease") is dated March 01, 2018, by and between Commercial building R us ("Landlord"), and MeshedTechs ("Tenant"). The parties agree as follows:

PREMISES. Landlord, in consideration of the lease payments provided in this Lease, leases to Tenant MeshedTechs (the "Premises") located at 1 main street, st. louis, Missouri 63012.

LEGAL DESCRIPTION. The legal description for the premises is: 10.977 square feet office space

TERM. The lease term will begin on March 01, 2018 and will terminate on March 01, 2019.

LEASE PAYMENTS. Tenant shall pay to Landlord monthly installments of $16,009.00, payable in advance on the first day of each month, for a total lease payment of $192,108.00. Lease payments shall be made to the Landlord at 123 any street, st. louis, Missouri 63102, which address may be changed from time to time by the Landlord.

POSSESSION. Tenant shall be entitled to possession on the first day of the term of this Lease, and shall yield possession to Landlord on the last day of the term of this Lease, unless otherwise agreed by both parties in writing. At the expiration of the term, Tenant shall remove its goods and effects and peaceably yield up the Premises to Landlord in as good a condition as when delivered to Tenant, ordinary wear and tear excepted. Landlord promises to place Tenant in peaceful possession of the Office Space, and Tenant, by taking possession of the Office Space, will have acknowledged that the Office Space are in satisfactory and acceptable condition. Landlord promises to place Tenant in peaceful possession of the Office Space, and Tenant, by taking possession of the Office Space, will have acknowledged that the Office Space are in satisfactory and acceptable condition.

USE OF PREMISES. Tenant may use the Premises only for office space and meetings The Premises may be used for any other purpose only with the prior written consent of Landlord, which shall not be unreasonably withheld. Tenant shall notify Landlord of any anticipated extended absence from the Premises not later than the first day of the extended absence.

PARKING. Tenant shall be entitled to use 75 parking space(s) for the parking of the Tenant's customers'/guests' motor vehicle(s).

STORAGE. Tenant shall be entitled to store items of personal property in in the basement totaling 500 square feet during the term of this Lease. Landlord shall not be liable for loss of, or damage to, such stored items.

PROPERTY INSURANCE. Landlord and Tenant shall each maintain appropriate insurance for their respective interests in the Premises and property located on the Premises. Landlord shall be named as an additional insured in such policies. Tenant shall deliver appropriate evidence to Landlord as proof that adequate insurance is in force issued by companies reasonably satisfactory to Landlord. Landlord shall receive advance written notice from the insurer prior to any termination of such insurance policies. Tenant shall also maintain any other insurance which Landlord may reasonably require for the protection of Landlord's interest in the Premises. Tenant is responsible for maintaining casualty insurance on its own property.

LIABILITY INSURANCE. Tenant shall maintain liability insurance on the Premises in a total aggregate sum of at least $25,000.00. Tenant shall deliver appropriate evidence to Landlord as proof that adequate insurance is in force issued by companies reasonably satisfactory to Landlord. Landlord shall receive advance written notice from the insurer prior to any termination of such insurance policies.

MAINTENANCE. Landlord shall have the responsibility to maintain the Premises in good repair at all times.

UTILITIES AND SERVICES.

Landlord shall be responsible for the following utilities and services in connection with the Premises:
- water and sewer
- garbage and trash disposal
- providing 24/7 building security

Tenant shall be responsible for the following utilities and services in connection with the Premises:
- electricity
- gas
- heating
- janitorial services
- telephone service
- Internet

Tenant acknowledges that Landlord has fully explained to Tenant the utility rates, charges and services for which Tenant will be required to pay to Landlord (if any), other than those to be paid directly to the third-party provider.

COMMON AREAS OF OFFICE SPACE. Landlord shall make available at all times during the term of this lease in any portion of the Office Space that Landlord from time to time designates or relocates, automobile parking and common areas as Landlord shall from time to time deem appropriate. Tenant shall have the nonexclusive right during the term of this lease to use the common areas for itself, its employees, agents, customers, clients, invitees, and licensees. Landlord reserves the right to re-designate a common area for a non-common use or to designate as a common area a portion of the Office Space not previously designated a common area.

All common areas shall be subject to the exclusive control and management of Landlord or any other persons or nominees that Landlord may have delegated or assigned to exercise management or control, in whole or in part, in Landlord's place and stead. Landlord shall have the right to close, if necessary, all or any portion of the common areas as is deemed necessary by Landlord to effect necessary repairs, maintenance, or construction, or to maintain the safety of tenants or the general public. Landlord will maintain the common areas in a clean, orderly, and sanitary manner. Landlord is responsible for all repairs of the common areas, except those required by the negligence of Tenant.

Landlord and Landlord's nominees and assignees shall have the right to establish, modify, amend, and enforce reasonable rules and regulations with respect to the common areas and the Office Space. Tenant shall fully and faithfully comply with and observe the rules and regulations for the common areas and the Building ("the Building Rules and Regulations"), of which the Leased Space is a part, including any additions or amendments to the Building Rules and Regulations that may be hereafter enacted by Landlord in Landlord's sole discretion.

PEST CONTROL. Tenant, at its sole expense, shall engage exterminators to control vermin and pests on a regular basis. Such extermination services shall be supplied in all areas where food is prepared, dispensed or stored and in all areas where trash is collected and deliveries are made.

JANITORIAL SERVICE. The Tenant shall provide regular janitorial service to the Leased Office Space at its sole expense.

COVENANT AGAINST WASTE. Tenant agrees that Tenant will not commit waste in or upon the Office Space or any portion thereof. The Tenant shall be responsible for the ventilation and cleanliness of the demised premises and for keeping the waste sewerage lines free from grease stoppages.

TAXES. Taxes attributable to the Premises or the use of the Premises shall be allocated as follows:

REAL ESTATE TAXES. Landlord shall pay all real estate taxes and assessments for the Premises.

PERSONAL TAXES. Landlord shall pay all personal taxes and any other charges which may be levied against the Premises and which are attributable to Tenant's use of the Premises, along with all sales and/or use taxes (if any) that may be due in connection with lease payments.

DESTRUCTION OR CONDEMNATION OF PREMISES. If the Premises are partially destroyed by fire or other casualty to an extent that prevents the conducting of Tenant's use of the Premises in a normal manner, and if the damage is reasonably repairable within sixty days after the occurrence of the destruction, and if the cost of repair is less than $50,000.00, Landlord shall repair the Premises and a just proportion of the lease payments shall abate during the period of the repair according to the extent to which the Premises have been rendered untenantable. However, if the damage is not repairable within sixty days, or if the cost of repair is $50,000.00 or more, or if Landlord is prevented from repairing the damage by forces beyond Landlord's control, or if the property is condemned, this Lease shall terminate upon twenty days' written notice of such event or condition by either party and any unearned rent paid in advance by Tenant shall be apportioned and refunded to it. Tenant shall give Landlord immediate notice of any damage to the Premises.

DEFAULTS. Tenant shall be in default of this Lease if Tenant fails to fulfill any lease obligation or term by which Tenant is bound. Subject to any governing provisions of law to the contrary, if Tenant fails to cure any financial obligation within 5 days (or any other obligation within 10 days) after written notice of such default is provided by Landlord to Tenant, Landlord may take possession of the Premises without further notice (to the extent permitted by law), and without prejudicing Landlord's rights to damages. In the alternative, Landlord may elect to cure any default and the cost of such action shall be added to Tenant's financial obligations under this Lease. Tenant shall pay all costs, damages, and expenses (including reasonable attorney fees and expenses) suffered by Landlord by reason of Tenant's defaults. All sums of money or charges required to be paid by Tenant under this Lease shall be additional rent, whether or not such sums or charges are designated as "additional rent". The rights provided by this paragraph are cumulative in nature and are in addition to any other rights afforded by law.

LATE PAYMENTS. For each payment that is not paid within 1 days after its due date, Tenant shall pay a late fee of $500.00 per day, beginning with the day after the due date.

CUMULATIVE RIGHTS. The rights of the parties under this Lease are cumulative, and shall not be construed as exclusive unless otherwise required by law.

NON-SUFFICIENT FUNDS. Tenant shall be charged $250.00 for each check that is returned to Landlord for lack of sufficient funds.

DANGEROUS MATERIALS. Tenant shall not keep or have on the Premises any article or thing of a dangerous, flammable, or explosive character that might substantially increase the danger of fire on the Premises, or that might be considered hazardous by a responsible insurance company, unless the prior written consent of Landlord is obtained and proof of adequate insurance protection is provided by Tenant to Landlord.

COMPLIANCE WITH REGULATIONS. Tenant shall promptly comply with all laws, ordinances, requirements and regulations of the federal, state, county, municipal and other authorities, and the fire insurance underwriters. However, Tenant shall not by this provision be required to make alterations to the exterior of the building or alterations of a structural nature.

ASSIGNABILITY/SUBLETTING. Tenant may not assign or sublease any interest in the Premises, nor effect a change in the majority ownership of the Tenant (from the ownership existing at the inception of this lease), nor assign, mortgage or pledge this Lease, without the prior written consent of Landlord, which shall not be unreasonably withheld.

GOVERNING LAW. This Lease shall be construed in accordance with the laws of the State of Missouri.

ENTIRE AGREEMENT/AMENDMENT. This Lease Agreement contains the entire agreement of the parties and there are no other promises, conditions, understandings or other agreements, whether oral or written, relating to the subject matter of this Lease. This Lease may be modified or amended in writing, if the writing is signed by the party obligated under the amendment.

SEVERABILITY. If any portion of this Lease shall be held to be invalid or unenforceable for any reason, the remaining provisions shall continue to be valid and enforceable. If a court finds that any provision of this Lease is invalid or unenforceable, but that by limiting such provision, it would become valid and enforceable, then such provision shall be deemed to be written, construed, and enforced as so limited.

WAIVER. The failure of either party to enforce any provisions of this Lease shall not be construed as a waiver or limitation of that party's right to subsequently enforce and compel strict compliance with every provision of this Lease.

BINDING EFFECT. The provisions of this Lease shall be binding upon and inure to the benefit of both parties and their respective legal representatives, successors and assigns.

SIGNATURES AND NOTICE. This Lease shall be signed by the following parties. No notice under this Lease shall be deemed valid unless given or served in writing and forwarded by mail, postage prepaid, addressed to the parties below:

LANDLORD:

Commercial building R us
Owner
123 any street
st. louis, Missouri 63102

TENANT:

MeshedTechs

Such addresses may be changed from time to time by either party by providing notice as set forth above. Notices mailed in accordance with the above provisions shall be deemed received on the third day after posting.

LANDLORD:

Commercial building R us

By: _____ Date: March 01, 2018
    Randy Arcega,
    Owner

TENANT:

_____ Date: March 01, 2018
MeshedTechs

Office furniture for those 60 employees

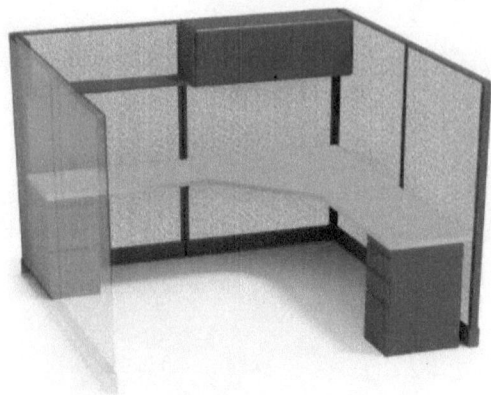

Total cost of furniture:

60 cubicles	$ 95,790.00
69 chairs	$ 15,318.00
3 conference tables	$ 8,154.00
	$ 119,262.00
	-$2,807,892.00
	$2,688,630.00

Computer equipment and Internet service into the building

Total cost of computer equipment and internet service for the building
60 Laptops with accessories $ 90,807.60
4 x 42U Server Cabinet Enclosure $ 6,335.72
2 x Full T1 internet connection with VoIP plus installation for 1 year $ 5,088.00
24 servers, 8 switches, 8 UPS battery backup systems, fiber and cat6 cables $
488,782.80

$ 591,014.12
-$ 2,688,630.00
=$ 2,097,615.88

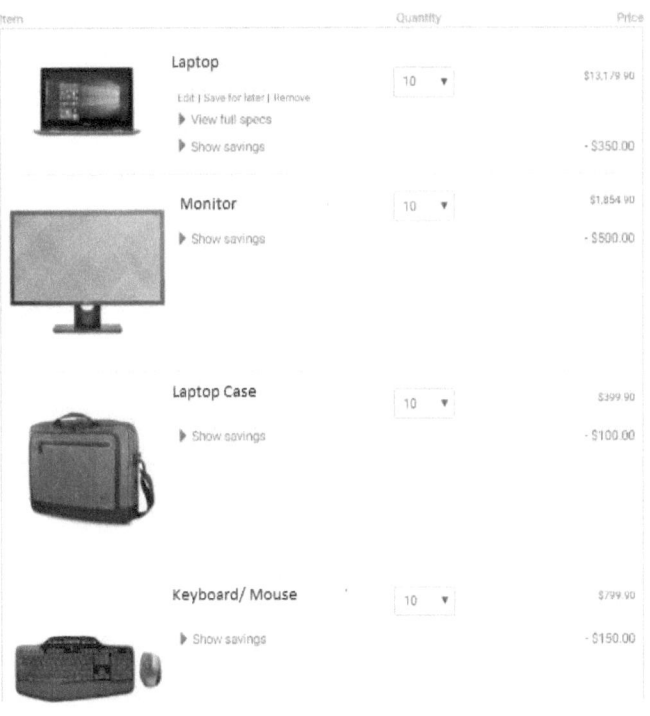

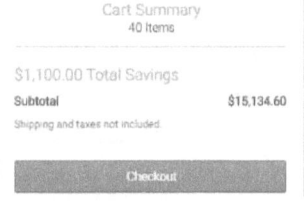

Item		Quantity	Price
Laptop		10 ▾	$13,179.90
Edit | Save for later | Remove			
▶ View full specs			
▶ Show savings			- $350.00
Monitor		10 ▾	$1,854.90
▶ Show savings			- $500.00
Laptop Case		10 ▾	$399.90
▶ Show savings			- $100.00
Keyboard/ Mouse		10 ▾	$799.90
▶ Show savings			- $150.00

Cart Summary
40 Items

$1,100.00 Total Savings

Subtotal $15,134.60

Shipping and taxes not included

Checkout

Interview and hire 45 extra highly
skilled programmers Interview and hire
6 excellent sales professionals

Recruiting service for 45 highly skills programmers	$ -900,000.00
Recruiting service for 6 sales professionals	$ -60,000.00
	$+$2,097,615.88
=	$1,137,615.88

Purchase a service that allows for the backup

and restore of company data for 1 year	$ 126,000.00
	-$1,137,615.88
	=$1,011,615.88

500 TB per month = $ 10,500.00

Pay your 60-person staff a salary for the year	$ 5,430,000.00
-	$ 1,011,615.88
=	$ 4,418,384.12

DON'T spend all the money in the first 4 quarters. (1 year)

So, things didn't go as planned, you need to either cut the costs or go back to the
investors and ask for another 4.5 million dollars.
Let us look at what we can do to cut the costs:

60 cubicles	$95,790.00	10 cubicles	$15,965.00
69 chairs	$415,318.00	18 chairs	$3,996.00
3 conference tables	$8,154.00	1 conference table	$2,718.00
60 laptops with accessories	$90,807.60	11 Laptops with accessories	$16,648.06
4x 42U Server Cabinet Enclosure	$6,335.72		
2x Full T1 internet connection with VOIP plus installation for 1 year	$5,088.00	1x Full T1 internet connection with VOIP plus installation for 1 year	$2,544.00

~~24 servers, 8 switches, 8 UPS battey~~
~~backup systems, fiber and~~

~~cat6 cables~~	~~$488,782.80~~	Windows Cloud service	$138,758.40
~~Recruiting service for~~		Recruiting service for	
~~45 highly skilled~~		1 highly skilled	
~~programmers~~	$900,000.00	programmer	$100,000.00
~~Recruiting service~~		Recruiting service	
~~for 6 sales professionals~~	$60,000.00	for 1 sales professional	$10,000.00

Purchase a service that allows for the backup and restore
of company data for 1 year $126,000.00

Pay your 60-person		Pay your 11-person	
staff a salary		staff a salary	
for the year	$5,430,000.00	for the year	$1,150,000.00

Expenses = $1,593,229.46
SeriesA funding = $3,000,000.00
New Total = $1,406,770.54

We reduced our staff requirements from 60 to 11, our vision is to grow the company as needed and with zero debt after the first year.

Chapter 8. Identifying the Vision for your IT Company

We gave you an idea about starting your own company in Chapter 7. (Work for yourself while working for your company), Now let's talk about some of the things to consider, and form a strategy for your business.

So, you're an IT person now and want to make some extra money with your new skill. Congratulations! First, that is a great achievement.

Start thinking about ideas you have to let your imagination go with anything. Go ahead and write down your list.

Organize these ideas into 3 categories: Ideas that I want to

Experience	Integrate into my personality	Purchase

Now that you have stated what you want, write out a contract for what you are going to give in return.

For example

Before November 1, 2018 I will have in my bank account the sum of $ 8 million 6 hundred 13 thousand 1 hundred 74our dollars and zero cents. In return for this money, I intend to create a software program that will serve 41,016 people in 12 states and 2 provinces in Canada and save them time.

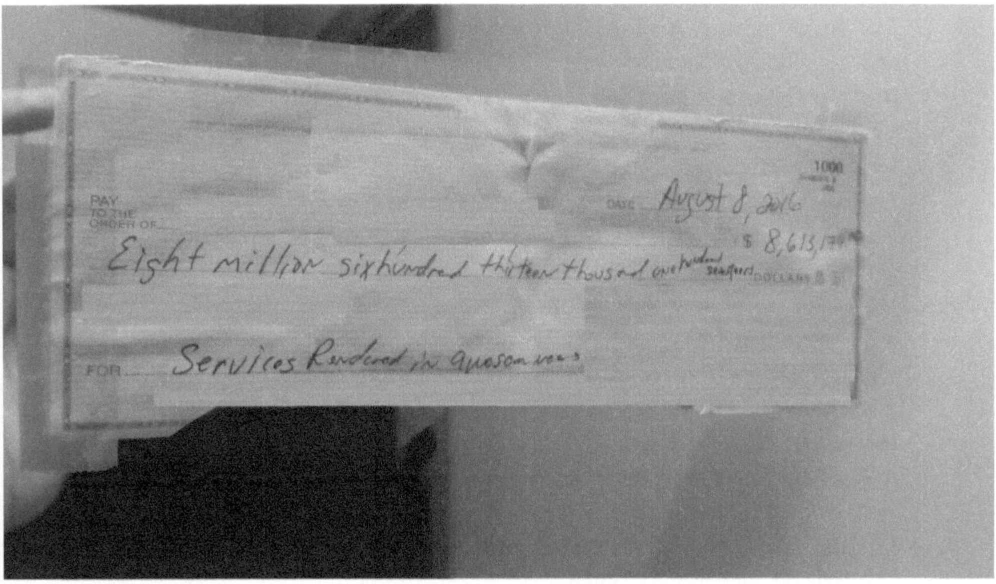
1000
PAY TO THE ORDER OF
DATE August 8, 2016
Eight million sixhundred thirteen thousand
DOLLARS
FOR Services Rendered

The next step is to create a plan for your IT business, this will tell the story about your business

1. Executive summary, this is a high-level description of your company and its products or services
2. Business Description, tell the story of your company
3. Market and Competition, talk about who is going to buy your product or service and who is your competition
4. Product or Service, talk about what you are selling
5. Management and Personnel, this is where you get to brag about the people in your company
6. Marketing and Selling, describe how you're going to get your brand in front or customers
7. Financial Data, this is the current or projected profit-and-loss or P&L statement. Most times investors will skip to this section first.
8. Investment, this is how much profit your investors can expect as a return.
9. Appendices, this can be testimonials from customers, An example of an Executive summary:
10. Milca's Playgroup is a kid's developing school, where the parents can enroll their children and have peace of mind.

An example of the Business Description:

Milca's Playgroup offers baby care for newborns (under 2 yrs.) and pre-school (2 ½ to 4 ½ yrs.) which provides activities that are designed to help the working parents to develop balance, coordination, and other sensory stimuli while having fun to also make the kids ready for school.

We designed activities according to their age to stimulate their learning skills with special toys and interactive games. Our facility has equipment for physical activities with a combination of imagination where the children will construct stories, draw, color, and do clay shaping. Listening skills and body awareness grow as the children explore the playscapes, create roles and predict outcomes. In addition, Milca's Playgroup offers a catering service for hosting children's parties, providing great activities for kids and parents. An enthusiastic Milca's Playgroup certified staff member leads the activities where their parents and friends play, laugh, and sing together creating a memorable experience.

An example of the Product or Service:

Milca's Playgroup offers hourly and monthly babysitting of children from newborn onwards. We have experts in the field of childcare on our staff to ensure the children have a safe environment. We prepare and serve meals (included with the baby care products) and will make arrangements for children with allergies.

Milca's Playgroup hours are from 7am to 11:30pm Monday through Friday. 7am to 5pm Saturday and Sunday

Our baby care products and rates are:

baby care hourly is $49.99 for the first 3 hours and $29.99 each additional hour. Baby Care monthly is $2,399.99 for unlimited hours each month

Chapter 9. Interview and Job Search Strategies that Work

The moment you start looking for a job is when you already have one, always be look for another job as you never know when your company will go out of business or lay you off.

Here are a couple of strategies that have worked for me and others, and it may benefit you as well.

1. Create a free email with your name in it. For example:

   firstname.lastname@domainname.com

2. Create a free blog such as Wordpress.com.
3. Create posts about your professional experience, post your resume and create an ABOUT ME page.
4. Create a free professional profile on Twitter, YouTube, LinkedIn and Instagram.
5. Create a YouTube video of what you know about in the IT field, talking about your experience or a "how to do something IT related" video.
6. Create your own money map, you are trading in your $14.00-hour Technical support job where you work from home in Chesterfield for a $20.00-hour Help Desk job where you work in an office in St. Louis from 9am to 5pm.

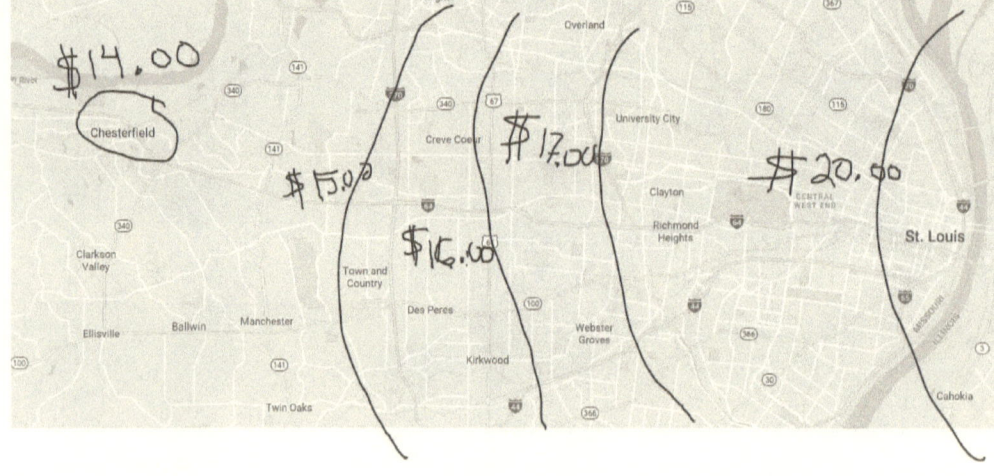

Things to consider when looking for a job in another location is your travel time and how that affects your family.

If your plan is to go from a work-from-home job to a job where you work in the office, calculate the amount of time you spend commuting and give that a dollar amount.

Example:

Current Job	Commute time daily	New Job	Real $ per hour amount	
$ 14.00	2 hours	$ 20.00 hr.	$ 18.00 hr.	
$ 14.00	1 hour	$ 16.00 hr	$ 15.00 hr	
$ 14.00	10 minutes	$ 15.00 hr	$ 15.00 hr	

Based on this you would tell any potential jobs with a 2 hour commute each day that your rate is at least $ 20.00 per hour

Here are a couple of strategies that have worked for others and me; it may benefit you as well.

1. Create your own list to track the job boards and companies you have put your resume on, research and KNOW what your target rate is for a given area and for each job board.

URL	Username	Password	Resume	Cover Letter	Target job	Target rate	Target Location
www.indeed.com	Username	Password	3/25/2018	3/25/2018	Help Desk	$ 20.00	St. Louis, MO
www.ziprecruiter.com	Username	Password	3/25/2018	3/25/2018	Help Desk	$ 20.00	St. Louis, MO
www.dice.com	Username	Password	3/25/2018	3/25/2018	Help Desk	$ 20.00	St. Louis, MO
www.hired.com	Username	Password	3/25/2018	3/25/2018	Help Desk	$ 40.00	Chicago, IL
Google.com	Search	For	Jobs	With the	Keyword	Help Desk	In St. Louis, MO

2. Create a phone call and interview-tracking list, this should include;
   a. Who is calling you?
   b. What is the location of the job they are calling about?
   c. What is the hourly/yearly rate THEY told you the job pays?
   d. What is the hourly/yearly rate YOU told them you wanted?
   e. What are the job requirements… degree, IT certificate, etc.?
   f. What was your voice tone during the conversation?
   g. Do you think you got the job?
   h. Do you think they will pay you more?
   i. If it was a face to face, what did their body language tell you?

3. Record every phone call and interview you go on, the reason being:

a. Listen to your voice tone, does it sound pleasing
b. Listen to the way you talk about yourself, does it say confidence
c. Listen to what you say about yourself, is there a way to get your point across in less words
d. Listen and write down if they talk about any duties not listed in the job description, LEARN THESE.
e. Write down and use a mechanism to remember their names, add them to LinkedIn immediately after

4. When talking to recruiters;
   a. make sure they know what hourly/yearly rate you expect to earn
   b. if they push back and tell you that the client is not willing to pay that, stand your ground and back it up with data from salary.com
   c. if you call a recruiter on Thursday, you have a great conversation and on Friday they don't know who you are, go to another recruiting company or apply to the client directly yourself
   d. search your recruiter on LinkedIn you will quickly find out if they got hired because of their looks or their technical experience
   e. Unless you believe you have a great chance of getting a job through them, don't spend time going to lunch with a recruiter, use this time learning or looking for a job.
   f. Don't give the recruiter any information they can use to get their friend the job, they are also your competition

5. Create a strategy to look through job posts.
   a. Start by going to the job board and search for Help Desk in St. Louis, MO

6. Create a strategy to look through job posts
   a. Open the job and break down the requirements
   b. Cross off the company jargon and benefits
   c. You're left with core functions of the job, go line by line, cross off and color the items GREEN that are related to skills you have acquired
   d. Make notes of what you need to learn

What		Where
help desk	Q	St. Louis, MO
Job Title, Keywords Or Company		City, State, Or Zip

Upload your resume - Let employers find you

Help Desk Specialist

- ★★★★☆ 2 reviews - St. Louis, MO

Analyzing workflow, access, information, and security requirements; Respond to email messages for customers seeking help....

Easily apply

Help Desk Specialist

~~Company is an industry leader in developing integrated marketing campaigns that simply and accurately communicate the right message at the right time. We specialize in strategy development, creative services, data analysis and production in order to create and manage successfully innovative programs from start to finish for our partners around the world.~~

Provide technical assistance and support for incoming queries and issues related to computer systems, software, and hardware. > **LEARN**

Respond to queries either in person or over the phone.

Maintain daily performance of computer systems.

Respond to email messages for customers seeking help. Walk customer through problem-solving process.

Install, modify, and repair computer hardware and software. Clean up computers and network drives > **LEARN** Run diagnostic programs to resolve problems.

Resolve technical problems with Local Area Networks (LAN), Wide Area Networks (WAN), and other systems. > **LEARN**

Install computer peripherals for users. > **LEARN**

Follow up with customers and users to ensure issue has been resolved. Gain feedback from customers about computer usage.

Run reports to determine malfunctions that occur. > **LEARN**

Train computer users.

Participate in network specifications by conferring with users; analyzing workflow, access, information, and security requirements; router administration, including interface configuration and routing protocols > **LEARN**

Monitor network performance issues including availability, utilization, throughput, and latency; planning and executing the selection, installation, configuration, and testing of equipment; establishing connections and firewalls > **LEARN**

Maintain network performance by performing network monitoring and analysis, and performance tuning; troubleshooting network; escalating problems to CISO > **LEARN**

Secure network by developing network access, monitoring, control, and evaluation; maintaining documentation > **LEARN** Upgrade network by conferring with vendors; developing, testing, evaluating, and installing enhancements > **LEARN** Proven experience and success with LAN, WAN design and implementation > **LEARN**

Proven experience with network capacity planning, network security principles, and general network management best practices > **LEARN**

Technical knowledge of network hardware, protocols, and Internet standards > **LEARN**

Excellent hardware troubleshooting experience > **LEARN**
Competence with testing tools and procedures for voice and data circuits > **LEARN**
Understanding of Cisco Network
equipment > **LEARN** Understanding of
LAN and WAN networking (TCP/IP) >
LEARN Understanding of vulnerability
detection/management > **LEARN** Strong
problem solving and communication skills
Self-driven and highly
motivated Strong
customer service
orientation The ability to
work in a team
environment
Willingness to work flexible hours — after hours
troubleshooting is occasionally required Minimum CCNA
Certification or higher (CCNP preferred) > **LEARN**
~~We offer: Competitive compensation and benefits, including medical, dental, vision, 401K, flexible spending, short and long term disability and life insurance.~~
~~Ongoing opportunities for development and career advancement based on merit.~~ Experience:
Network Administrative: 1 year
(Required) > **LEARN**
Education: Associate (Required) > **LEARN**
License or certification: CCNA Certification or Higher (Required) > **LEARN**

7. Create a return on Job Investment for each job you apply for if you need more education or a certification

Example:
The job title is Help Desk Specialist, pays $28.00 per hour

Your current job pays $14.00 per hour
The job requires an Associate's Degree. It is a two-year time investment, cost $9,000.00. The job requires CCNA. It is a three-month time investment, cost $250.00

$ 14.00 x 2080 hours in a year x 2 years before taxes	$58,240.00
salary Associates degree	- $9000.00
CCNA	- $250.00
	= $48,990.00

Question: If you get a spend 3 months and get a CCNA, what type of job can you get? Answer: $ 29.00 per hour

DON'T MAKE THE MISTAKE by thinking that you need to pay $ 9,000 to get a degree for a job that just requires a $ 250 certification.

Chapter 10. Research the Company

If you have a strong lead then you need to learn the company structure, key players, and their duties before the interview. You can get most of the information for a competent interview from the company website. See if they have a directory that list people in the department you are applying. Things to consider looking up and committing to memory could be things like:

- History of the Organization

- Details of what the company does or sells

- Size of the organization

- Location/Address of the main office(s)

- Main departments and the heads of those departments

- The mission statement or the "Why" of the organization

It may also benefit you to look at the company's financial history and economic outlook from various investments sites to get an idea of where the company fits in the financial world and who their competitors may be in similar markets.

Gathering Company Info

Other than the main company's website, your best tool to find out information about the company is by using search engines. Using engines like Google or Bing can often turn up more information that you can get from just visiting the company website. You may even find out things that will make you look very knowledgeable in the interview. Perhaps you are applying for a technical position and find that they use a certain version of Linux, you could then review that particular Linux flavor and drop in some details specific to the version.

Google has some powerful tools at that you can help fine tune your searches. It may surprise you to learn that Google maintains not only current information about websites but the history of them too. If you would like to search its cache and not the current version then just type **cache:<website name>** in the search bar, for example:

Google and the Google logo are registered trademarks of Google LLC, used with permission

Another good shortcut to finding out about relationships the organization has would be the **link** operator. The **link** operator will return any webpages that contain links to the site you specify in the query. To use this tool, you simply type **link:<website name>** in the search bar. See example below.

link:contoso.com

Google Search   I'm Feeling Lucky

One of the best and most often used Google operators has to be the site search. The site search will restrict the search just to the specified location or domain. The syntax of this command is a little different from the previous two. With this operator you also have to list the search words you want to use and then tell google to limit the search to a specific site:

\<keyword> site:\<website name>

office address site:contoso.com

Google Search   I'm Feeling Lucky

The search refinements listed here are by no means exhaustive and while it may be a bit of an overkill to go to deep into a large company's site you may want to further explore Google's capabilities by going to https://support.google.com/websearch/answer/2466433?hl=en or by simply searching for google operators in a search bar.

Don't limit yourself to just one search engine. When you use just one engine, you risk severely limiting the results you can get. Different engines index information differently based on how they tend to weigh what they find important. Also remember that some popular engines are really just front ends to other more powerful engines. For example, Yahoo! has used many different engines to power their searches over the years while maintaining a common website. I personally like to use Google, Bing, and DuckDuckGo when trying to gather website data.

Gathering People Info

Getting information on key people in the organization or at least the department head and leads of the section for which you are applying can be beneficial. Maybe they went to the same college as you or like the same activities you do, perhaps you grew up near each other or run in the same circles. These commonalties can help you feel more relaxed in an interview and ease the transitions between interview points. Being relatable will also help you be more memorable and at the very least it may help each party involved feel more optimistic about being on the new team when hired.

There are many ways to get information about a person. I would stay away from using sites or services that gather information on people that they have not shared on their own. Acquiring data that people did not explicitly share themselves is a sure way to make someone wary of you if they found out, or at least feel uncomfortable around you. Even "social media stalking" can be a bit invasive for some. Chances are that if people publicly post information about themselves then it is acceptable to look at the data or is at least an easily forgivable offense. Listed below are some of the most popular ways people are sharing details about themselves and their lives, with a brief description about the service:

Instagram This media service allows people to share photos and videos with others. The service allows users to apply various filters to their digital media. The videos and photos are organized with tags and location data content can be shared publicly or limited to certain accounts. It was bought by Facebook Inc in 2012.

Facebook One of the largest social networks on paper, Facebook claims a very large user base. Along with individual user accounts, groups can also be created that let users share common interests. Other benefits to this service are the ability to sign on to participating websites and the ability to leave comments on other sites using your Facebook account details.

Glassdoor While not strictly a social media site, Glassdoor is a good resource to see reviews and salaries of large companies. If you want to get an idea of what a company is paying someone in a similar position that you are applying for then this site can give you a ballpark figure. Please remember that salaries should just be used as a guide and should not be used as a strict model for your compensation package.

LinkedIn One of the best professional social media sites currently available. This service was designed to be collaborative for professionals looking for jobs and for many is used as an online resume. You can find a lot of relevant information about a person here such as their past employers, contact information, skills, professional network, etc.

Twitter This media service has a large number of users as well, and many of them make several posts a day. Twitter allows people to create short messages on any number of topics with little regard to controlling who sees the feeds. With this service you can see what a particular person is following and get great insight into their interests and thoughts.

If the company you are applying to is small or you cannot find much information about them online then you can always call the main phone number and start asking questions. There is no reason to be secretive about what you are trying to do. You can call in and ask them whatever questions you feel are relevant to pursuing the job. Ask about the various departments within the company, the heads of the departments, and if you find someone willing to talk in depth and is very knowledgeable, then you could even consider asking about the various dispositions of the people that are going to interview you. If the person you first speak with is unable or unwilling to discuss the details that you wish to know, then ask to be transferred to someone else who can give you more info. Just remember being proactive is a good thing but being invasive and taking too much of someone's time can be a bad thing, especially if there are hundreds of candidates, many of which may be doing the same thing.

Chapter 11. The Interview

After you have researched the company and department you are applying to then you need to start crafting well thought out questions based on the facts you have gleaned. Try to find a good time during the interview to interject the questions into the conversation. Almost all interviewers, at some point, should provide you with an opportunity to ask your own questions. If you haven't had the chance during the natural course of the interview to show that you are driven to getting the position with your well researched questions, then wait until you are asked if "you have any questions" for them.

Practice the questions you came up with aloud. Try to imagine some of the questions that they will ask you. Look online for common interview questions for your particular field. Make sure things are spoken as you would in the interview, just do not go through the interview in your head. Sometimes getting the message from your head to your mouth is a little tricky when you feel pressure or are unsure about a specific point. Practicing the actual words and cadence of your spoken thoughts will go a long way in to creating a fluid interview.

Knowing the company is not the only thing you should be studying: you should also know yourself and your resume. This may seem like a common-sense statement but it isn't all too obvious if you really want to nail down your abilities. Have you thought about how your work history fits into this particular company and the job for which you are applying? Are there things not in your resume that are relevant? Most people build a generic resume that shows a high-level overview of themselves. Before the interview, start to consider what your resume says and how the interviewer will see you just based on that. Perhaps you were an administrator that "did other duties as assigned." Many times, those other duties, while not so important at your last job are the exact thing(s) that this potential employer is looking for.

It was covered earlier, but know the description of the job you are applying for. Try to get a feel for the department and what they want out of a candidate by reading between the lines. Remember examples of the times you had experiences with the types of things they want. If you don't have some of the experience, think of ways that you could get them, review the basic ideas and concepts of what they are looking for but don't have experience with. You may find that while you don't have the exact experience that they want, you may have very similar experience with something else.

Make sure you come prepared to an interview. Often more than one person will be present to interview you and it could very well be a panel of people. The more people that show up to your interview the higher the chance that someone will not have a copy of your resume; make sure you have several extra copies. A bottle of water, a pen, and notepad should also be some things to consider bringing with you to an interview. Write down the names of the people who interviewed you and what they do in the company: this will help if you are called back for further interviews. The day or night before the interview make sure you know how to get there by actually going there. It may even be best to do your dry run around the same time you will have to leave for your interview so you will get an idea of what kind of traffic you will have to endure.

Be confident and social in the interview. Pretend that you are already friends with the interviewers. If you have done your homework by this point you should know something about the people you are going to be talking to about the potential job. Try to focus on your commonalties in your mind, organically bring them up in the interview. Have a firm handshake and smile as you make eye contact. Be mindful to make eye contact throughout the interview as well. Eye contact is one of the best nonverbal tools you have. It lets people know you are confident and you have good self-esteem. It also lets others know that you are a social person and can work well with others. Eye contact when you are listening is as important as when you are speaking, it lets someone know you are actively engaged in what they have to say and are interested in what they have to say. Other things you can do to project confidence is to sit up straight and keep a pleasant demeanor. Ask intelligent questions or give insightful commentary on the topic that the interviewer is covering. Make sure your words are clear and at an appropriate level, project your words.

Always be truthful. Many people think that they are good liars or pad their resumes with things that are not technically true. Even a decent interviewer can usually spot at least one or two embellishments and most often that is all it takes to disregard a candidate. Always tell the truth. If you don't know something, say you don't know and try to think of ways on how you could learn, or what you can do to compensate. Don't say something like, "I used to do it a long time ago but don't remember too much about it now." Most often all it takes is one question to find its way through a fraudulent statement. Once something like that happens, interviews are quick to end and you will probably never get the real feedback on why you didn't get the position.

After the interview, be sure to follow up quickly. Decisions are usually made fast, and sending an email the next day to the interviewer could tip the decision in your favor if the competition was close. Do not make the follow up too long, perhaps less than a page. Make sure you thank the interviewer and remind them how you believe you would help the group or organization. If you haven't heard anything in about two weeks considering sending another email or calling to let him or her know you are still interested in the position. If the job has already been filled ask if they can provide feedback on what you could have done better or what you can do to be more competitive when you apply for similar jobs in the future.

Some questions should not be asked during the interview. Do not discuss pay or benefits (including vacation) with the interviewer. The best time to ask these types of questions is with the recruiter, if you have one, or if you are offered the position. Also, do not ask about how many hours you will be required to work. Keep in mind that interviews are to find a candidate that is best suited to fill a particular function that the company has a deficit in. Questions that focus around, or imply the desire to not do the job are red flags. Asking how long until you are able to get a promotion also shows that you aren't interested in the job you are applying to, as much as you are to move beyond it. Remember, the interviewer needs someone to do a job. They aren't looking for someone that is trying to get their foot in the door so that they can quickly move on.

Other not so obvious questions not to ask start with "Why". Some why questions sound like accusations and can make people feel uncomfortable even if it is at a subconscious level. Try to reword your why question with a more positive spin. "Why do you use cubicles" could be reworded as "Do cubicles provide better efficiency with the company's work flow?"

Asking about work schedules is another topic best left for the pre-interview or post offer. Work-life balance is an important aspect of any job and is a popular buzzword, but hiring decision makers do not make that a priority. It gives the impression that you are more concerned about your time and self than with the direction of the company. Realistically, most people are very much more concerned about themselves or their families, and rightfully so for the most part, but it is not appropriate to make it so obvious.

Another popular trend that should be avoided in conversation during the interview is working from home. If a job allows it, then the job description usually will imply such a thing. If not, once again, the interview is not the place to start negotiating a work from home solution. Some companies will allow it once you have established that you can be trusted to actually work from home. Many will also have a grace period before you can even consider working from home. Remember it takes time to get a feel for a company and the way they do things. Just because you know the job already does not mean you know the intimate details of a company. If you are lucky enough to find a job that lets you work from home then use your office work "probation" to get to know the people that you will have to work with or may have to work with in the future. Find out about the resources available to once you start working from home. Learn the culture and "cadence" of the company and what is expected of you.

The interview process is about selling yourself for a particular position. It is about letting the interviewer(s) know what you can do for them, it is not about finding out what a company can do for you. Keep this in mind during the whole process. If the company finds that they value your potential contribution then you can start negotiating things like time off, or work schedules. Most of the time the people who interview you are not the same ones who are providing the benefits so don't be shy about what you want once it gets to that stage. Of course, if the job is at a smaller company then it may very well be the same people, and you might need to exercise more caution. By knowing the company and your worth to them, you will be better prepared to get the job you want.

Chapter 12. Increase your Online Presence

Now that you have gone over all the important steps to finding a job, we can finally come to the "meta" strategy for finding a job. Why do I use the term "meta"? In this case "meta" will refer to the Greek word "meta" which is a prefix meaning "after" or "beyond" and not a self-referencing colloquialism. It is the level beyond the level at which you are conceptualizing. The concept that has our attention is of finding a job, so the "meta" job is having an online presence. Many recruiters and interviewers will often seek out information from online sources about a candidate. Depending on the job, an online presence maybe a necessity or it may be just something that gives you a slight edge if done properly. Of course, it could mean nothing, and any edge can become double-sided in that if you project the wrong persona on a social site it may even hurt your chances at landing the right job.

Many people today will stress the importance of having an online footprint and often stress being on many social sites as imperative to finding a job. I tend to believe that while it can be useful to have a respectful online presence you can get a job (even in IT) with having just one or two accounts if any at all. Most of the jobs I have worked over the years took very little consideration of my profile and most likely recruiters are going to rely on social accounts more than the interviewer for a large company. Keeping an online resume with just the facts and some references may be one of the easiest and best strategies when it comes to "being online." That and scrubbing your other accounts for anything that may be considered offensive and alludes that you may be someone who would rather party than work. Remember you are selling yourself as a hard worker and someone who will care about the company's wellbeing before your own.

Say you do want more than just an online resume; well, let us go over some basics. If you are a professional, your best strategy is to maintain a professional presence. Sites like LinkedIn, GadBall, Meetup, Opportunity, and other such sites are geared towards having a professional place for people to help develop a community of workers. Most of these sites will help connect like-minded professionals and can often help users get a clearer picture of the industry and the people in them. If you stay up to date you can often derive trends, connect with recruiters, and get advice from leaders in numerous fields. Keep your profile professional and limit opinions on topics not related to your desired profession. It should go without saying but I am going to say it anyway: comments about drinking/drugs, parties, or how you feel about the current state of politics and religion are best left for other mediums of communication.

So, you created your social media accounts, now what? How do you get people to your site or profile? How do you keep them and grow your influence? The most important thing you can do is to actively and sincerely engage with people. If you joined several social sites and just expect to collect followers or friends with little interaction, then after some time you may find people have disconnected from your profile or perhaps you are just connected to the other "ghost" accounts that yours has become. The purpose of a social media account is to be social and you need to be sincere and interesting to have a robust following. It should be more fulfilling to have fifty engaged contacts then five hundred inactive accounts hanging off your profile.

- Make sure to reply to comments or mentions in a timely manner
- Add people to your comments or discussion; really try to engage a wide audience even if it just started out as a conversation between you and one other person. People really like to give their opinions on varied topics even if they don't know too much about something; just validating their opinions right or wrong can go a long way.
- Try to answer questions that are asked of you promptly.
- Limit your reposts. If you do not add any value to a post made by someone else then try not to make it a habit of being the person who just reposts (retweets) things they find interesting or amusing.
- Stay positive. If there is a difference of opinion on a topic, it does not have to turn into an argument. Two sides of an issue can be intelligently discussed without it devolving into something like a text based screaming match. If you find that the other person is getting upset try to diffuse the negative interchange. This usually means you have to give more concessions than you feel justified in doing but the reality is that if someone is entrenched enough in their opinion to get upset and lose focus on presenting reasonable counterpoints then they are not in a mindset to accept your points anyway. It is best to politely move on.
- Add new content consistently. If you just post intermittently people may think that the social connection may not be worthwhile. Of course, if you post too much it may be overwhelming especially if the content isn't that interesting to your audience. Try to find a good middle ground. If you do happen to be a very interesting and involved person, then there may not be such a thing as too much. You may have to gauge your feedback to get an idea of what is interesting and engaging and what is not. I once belonged to a news aggregate site that had a very prolific comment section. In fact, the comment section was often where most people spent their time and also added to the information in the articles, so much so that the authors of the articles would make numerous revisions based on the comments. It took me at least a year to understand the flow and mindset of the group. Although there were tens of thousands of members, after some time and any contributions, I was able to perceive a give and take, and understand all the unwritten rules. Of course, after fifteen years I realized that perhaps they were not my audience after all.

Know your audience. Outline your goals for having an online social life. What do you want out of it? Once you start to understand your reasons for creating an online life then try to match an audience to your goals. Are you a thrill seeker looking to connect with people who found that next adrenaline fix? Then it would not make a lot of sense if you were to reach out to people who are shopping for insurance with a toothpick splinter clause. Find groups on the big social media sites and look for people who contribute content to the discussions, ask them to be your friends. Find websites with your similar interests and see if that website sponsors any groups that you can become a member of. Do not limit yourself to online groups, go out and find like-minded people, add them to your digital collection.

The most popular medium right now is video. Visual content is very engaging and it allows you to get your idea out quickly. If you have interesting content and make the critical points with something memorable, then video can be very effective at keeping you or your subject in the minds of people who see it. Most people post text and the amount of written content published daily is significant. If you really want to stand out, then a good way to do that is to make yourself a multimedia presence. When I was younger, I once applied for a job in which the hiring manager asked if I knew the latest web animation software: I did not. I purchased one of those teach yourself in 24 hours books and sent him a web animation to his email the very next day showing him what I learned in the short time since the interview. I did not get the job because someone had turned in something much better, and their whole resume was a web animation and much more interactive than mine. I had been outdone, and I was impressed with their creativity: they were the better candidate, and I moved on.

Think of some ways you can make yourself more memorable to the hiring manager. They may see hundreds of applications a day. What are you doing to stand out? Sure, you could rely on the content of your resume, but many jobs value creative people. Maybe you don't have much work experience, so try to think of ways to make yourself stand out professionally.

Chapter 13. Give a Professional Appearance

While the proper dress for a job will vary from company to company there are a few guidelines that you can follow. Casual footwear such as sandals or tennis shoes should be avoided in a professional setting. Showing your undergarments or possibly revealing even more, distracts from selling yourself and your non-aesthetic assets. I am sure you could think of many jobs where this might be a helping point, but remember this is for the professional setting or jobs that will help you achieve a lasting career. So, things like shorts, jeans, short skirts, low cut anything, see through anything (except maybe glasses) are to be avoided.

If you have the opportunity, try to find out what the dress culture is like at the company you will be interviewing for. Keep in mind, however, that what they wear every day for work isn't the same thing that you should wear to an interview. Usually you dress up more for an interview. But if the company is really casual, let's say flip-flops are okay, then slacks and a nice shirt would be dressing up without over doing it.

Don't dress too out-dated. Whether conscious of it or not an interviewer will take into considerations many factors that have little to do with the job. If you do not have anything classic or modern then it would be a good time to invest in an interview outfit. Do not overlook the shows either. Both men and women will notice shoes alike. I have often been told that the two most observed things about them are their watches and their shoes. Of course, that adage may have changed with the newer generation but I suspect what one wears on their wrist and feet are still often critically observed with perhaps the only thing changing being what brand is considered to be in fashion. You don't have to spend a fortune on your outfit and you can find many brand name items at discount stores or even get nice non-name brand clothes at more affordable places.

As far as makeup goes, don't overdo it. You may think you don't wear a lot of makeup and maybe you don't but try asking some of your closest friends their opinion about how much makeup you wear. Be sure the person you ask isn't known to wear too much themselves. Also make sure to let your friends know that you want an honest answer, be clear to them that it would very much help you in your interview if they were honest and that you won't get mad. If you don't want to approach your friends then go to a mall or similar location where they do free makeup applications. Find someone that you feel doesn't have much if any makeup on and ask them what they use and then let them demonstrate how to apply a modest amount of makeup on you.

I have a friend who wears makeup like a mask, she would be perfectly at home at a carnival in just her everyday makeup. Over the years people have made polite comments about the amount she wears and that she would look just as pretty with a bit less. Subtle comments like these from friends should be a huge red flag that you are wearing too much makeup. Most people try to be as polite as possible on the subject of people's appearances, so even a very subtle comment from someone should be a clue to reevaluate your makeup choices. It took many comments from her friends and students for her to finally accept that maybe it was too much, but even today she more often than not will heavily apply the mask of makeup.

Along the lines of too much makeup is also too much cologne or perfume. I personally like the heavily scented aroma that masks the natural stenches of the human condition but there is a limit. Some people are more sensitive to smells than others. Some people have aversions to certain scents. What if one of the lab-created smells you applied to yourself dredged up bad memories from the hiring manager. Such things can work against you. Have a good bath or shower before the interview and apply a modest amount of fragrance, this way you won't negatively distract from the interview.

Don't come with too many accessories, that may be fine for toys but for an interview it is unprofessional. Too many rings, bracelets, necklaces, etc. aren't so much stylish as they are distracting. Make the interviewer interested in you and not the things you have purchased. Too big of accessories are also an interview no-no. Go for the classic subtle jewelry, this means one earing in each ear and nowhere else that can be seen. Many companies today aren't as willing to discard a candidate for excessive piercings or tattoos but in a professional environment it would be better to err on the side of conservative attire as there are still plenty of hiring managers who see such modifications as indicative of someone who they would rather pass on.

In one of my most current positions a young man was hired and he was an adequate candidate. As a folly of his youth he believed himself to be more capable than he was and therefore more indispensable, so he shed off his conservative mask and began dying his hair in various bright pastel colors every few weeks. While he was competent at his job this behavior left many on his team and in the office feeling that maybe he wasn't the best fit and wasn't actually that competent. Of course, what one does with their hair doesn't have much to do with their abilities but you need to be aware of the unconscious or conscious bias of many people. He was eventually told that he had to appear more professional or they would not be able to retain him any longer. He did end up going back to his natural color but he was quietly moved to the "b" team and many in the office still consider him towards the bottom of his peer group in abilities. He didn't know or at least didn't respect the culture and it will take a long time for him to cast off his immature quirk and lose the nicknames related to his coloring of his hair. Are the people who slighted him wrong? Perhaps, but as a candidate you shouldn't use your interview as a place to make your cultural opinions known.

Don't let your digital devices distract from the interview. Turn your cell phone off or at least put it on vibrate. Never answer your cell phone during an interview, or check your messages for that matter. If feel like you might have an emergency during the interview let the interviewer know beforehand that your phone is on and there may be an emergency that you will have to respond to. Also take off the headset, earbud, or whatever else that may look like you are not giving one hundred percent of your attention to the interviewer. Don't chew gum, or fidget with gadgets. If you are the nervous type then run through mock interviews until you can sit still and focus.

Chapter 14. Eat Smart Before the Interview

Whatever time of day your interview, is your day should start with a breakfast that stimulates your brain and body. Many people think a good and necessary start to their day is a cup of coffee, or two, or perhaps three. If that is your habit then you will need that caffeine to maintain your standard performance but I would not recommend going for that extra cup or two as it may end up leading you with a strong desire to relieve yourself at an inopportune time. The fact is if you require coffee to start your day then you have a physical addiction to caffeine, the day of your interview is no time to go cold turkey: get your fix. If you do not regularly consume caffeine as part of your daily ritual and you do not have any ethical objections to the practice then a standard dose of 70 – 140 mg of caffeine may help you stay alert and have a short-term positive impact on your memory. If you do not ingest caffeine often then I would suggest staying at the low end of your intake of caffeine for the day, say perhaps 40 – 70 mg.

A common misconception about caffeine is that it gives you a boost to wake you up after a night's rest. What actually happens is that once you become addicted, the caffeine perks you up to your natural state of alertness. The effects that were achieved when you first started dosing with caffeine get less and less effective for the same amount of caffeine. This means that you either have to take more to keep that original state of alertness or you keep taking the same amount till one day the effect just "takes the edge off" of the withdrawal. I am not advocating the benefit or drawbacks of caffeine, it is just important to know what is actually happening so you can better get to your peak performance for interview day.

Here are some other things to note about caffeine that may help you plan your interview strategy. The effects of caffeine tend to begin around twenty minutes of ingesting. It will help you be more alert and increase your concentration. After about three hours, the effect will wear out. A good window is to take your caffeine about an hour before a situation in which you want to benefit from its effects. For some people caffeine, as in coffee, can act as a laxative. If you do not know how you react to caffeine, right before an interview would not be a good time to experiment.

"So, if I do not use caffeine to get me alert, then what?" The best thing to naturally wake you up can arguably be apple juice, but any juice without added sugar and a good amount of vitamin C will be fine. Note:, it is not the vitamin C that we're looking for in a drink; the drinks that provide the precursors the body needs usually have a healthy dose of vitamin C, think citrus juices.

Along with the juice make sure you get some protein. Try not to eat heavy foods for your protein. Eggs, milk, or light yogurt are good options. Remember moderation is the key, do not overdo your diet.

Fruits are always a good idea for a natural source of energy. Some fruits are more beneficial than others and you can't go wrong with apples of course. I know you have heard about what just one apple a day can do to doctors but have you heard this one? "If you aren't hungry enough to want an apple then you're not hungry." That is something to think about if you are about to start a diet, but for interview time eat whatever fruit you want.

Do not forget to add some veggies. Your B series vitamins along with folic acid always helps with your health and cognitive tasks. This will help fortify you in your quest to be alert and keep your brain firing on all cylinders.

Try to avoid some foods too. Too many carbohydrates can drag you down. Pastas, white rice, and certain cereals may not be your best friend for alertness and quick energy. Avoid foods with strong smells. Notice that I said strong smells and not bad smells. You do not know who you are going to interact with and what their food preferences are, do not get associated with a smell of a certain food. Also, stay away from any food that may make you want to have to use the bathroom quicker than normal for you. Everyone is different and hopefully you have a good idea of what foods cause undesired reactions to your normal routines.

On a final note, stay away from the sugar before the interview. Afterwards feel free to load up on gummy bears (as long as doing so does not go against the medical advisements.) In addition, if you feel the need to take something stronger than caffeine maybe you should sit down and reevaluate some things going on in your life. Some people may think prescription or illegal drug use can give them an edge over other candidates, and indeed some employers might see that level of energy as useful. However, remember the people who see that as beneficial most likely are the same people who would have no problem using you up until you are a barely functional husk. It is better to get a job based on your natural abilities than to "juice" for the interview.

www.ingramcontent.com/pod-product-compliance
Lightning Source LLC
Chambersburg PA
CBHW030524220526
45463CB00007B/2703